Published by
Gallery Books
An imprint of W H Smith Publishers Inc.
112 Madison Avenue
New York, New York 10016 USA

Produced by
Twin Books
15 Sherwood Place
Greenwich, CT 06830 USA

ISBN 0-8317-2301-7

Printed in Hong Kong

Fun with Words
At Home

Twin Books

GALLERY BOOKS
An imprint of W.H. Smith Publishers Inc.
112 Madison Avenue
New York, New York 10016

OUR HOUSE

Baby Mickey and his friends are building a house.

Baby Goofy has just put the  on top

to keep out the rain. He is pleased with the way

it looks, and he hasn't forgotten the 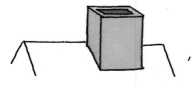 ,

either. The house is almost finished. Baby Goofy

will add a 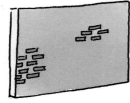 at the back and

Baby Mickey is about to put the

on the front. Baby Daisy and Baby Donald are

the gardeners. They have filled the box at the

 with beautiful flowers. Now they are

planting trees all around the house.

Door

Chimney

Roof

Wall

Window

OUR FRONT YARD

Baby Donald does not have to ring the .

Baby Daisy opened the door when she heard

his car outside on the front walk.

She is happy that all her friends have come

to visit. Baby Daisy waits on the

to let her friends in when they have climbed

the 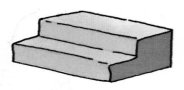 . Baby Mickey is so eager to

see everyone that he has left the

open. And no one has thought to look in the

 for letters even though the mailman

has already stopped at Baby Daisy's house.

Doorbell

Doormat

Steps

Gate

Mailbox

GROWING THINGS

Last spring, Baby Mickey planted a seed,

and now it has become a  .

Carefully, he tends his plant and touches

its new  . It is good to see things

growing, from the smallest flower to the

tallest shady  .

Baby Donald looks at his gardening book

while he rests beside a green

with his teddy bear. Baby Horace and Baby Gus

have filled their truck with  to take

to the farmer's market.

Bush

Tree

Flower

Leaf

Fruit

OUR BACK YARD

It is a bright sunny day, and Baby Minnie

is enjoying the  while she watches

Baby Pluto bury his bone beside his  .

Baby Pluto digs so many holes in the back yard

that the Babies have to keep a

by his house to make the lawn smooth and

neat again. Baby Mickey has been playing

with his pail and  , but now

Baby Pete decides that it's his turn. Instead of

asking, he squirts Baby Mickey with the  .

Poor Baby Mickey has lost his shovel !

Swing

Doghouse

Rake

Hose

Shovel

OUR PETS

Baby Goofy's favorite pet is a little

named Pluto, who always wants to play. Goofy

likes to push the ball to Pluto. Then Pluto pushes it

back. Baby Daisy and Baby Minnie love to hold their

pet  Button, who is soft and friendly.

Button hops straight to Baby Minnie when she

reaches for him. Pokey the  lets Baby

Mickey pull her around on the train set. The train

goes faster than she does! Meanwhile, Furry the

 has no one to play with, so she is

watching Finny the in his bowl.

14

Puppy

Rabbit

Turtle

Kitten

Fish

IN OUR LIVING ROOM

Baby Minnie is sitting up on a  so

she can show Baby Pete how to place the toy

furniture for company. She has put one of

her dolls in the  beside her, and

Baby Pete wants to put her other doll on the  .

Now who will get to rock in the  ?

Not Baby Donald, he's much too big.

Besides, he's too busy playing with his boats

to get ready for company. But the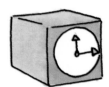

on the table shows that it's almost time for

the visitors to arrive !

.

Clock

Rocking Chair

Sofa

Chair

Cushion

IN OUR FAMILY ROOM

Today it's raining, so Baby Minnie and Baby

Mickey are playing indoors. First they watch a

cartoon on the  set. Now Baby

Minnie is pushing the buttons on her

to find some music that she likes. Baby Mickey

has searched the shelves for some of their

favorite picture  to look at. If they

want to draw, there is paper in the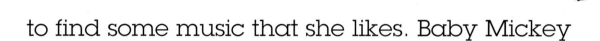

drawer and pencils beside the TV. Perhaps they

will copy the  of a barn that hangs

beside the bookcase.

Television

Picture

Desk

Radio

Book

OUR TOYS

The Disney Babies are very lucky to have so many

toys. Baby Minnie loves taking care of her

which has a hair bow just like hers and eyes that

open and shut. With a nice big  like

that, Baby Mickey can carry a lot of toys around.

"Whee !" yells Baby Donald on his  .

But Baby Goofy is too busy looking in the toy

box to pay attention. First he found a smiling

 , and now he is looking for something

else. Could it be the big striped on the

floor next to Baby Mickey's truck ?

Rocking Horse

Teddy
Bear

Doll

Truck

Ball

THINGS FOR QUIET PLAY

When it is cold, the Disney Babies like to play inside

and not make too much noise. Baby Mickey

can color in his  . He uses all the crayons

in the box. Baby Donald is making a chain of paper

figures. He folds the 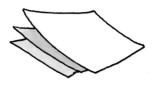 backwards

and forwards, then cuts around an outline with

a pair of  . Baby Daisy draws a

picture of Baby Mickey with a  .

Now she is getting ready to paint in the colors

with the 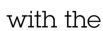 .

Sometimes it is fun to play quietly.

Pencil

Coloring Book

Paintbrush

Scissors

Paper

IN OUR KITCHEN

Baby Daisy and Baby Clarabelle have gotten up

early to make breakfast. They have some warm

milk to make hot chocolate on their toy  .

Baby Daisy pours some into the cups, while Baby

Gyro tries to figure out how the toast pops out of

the  . Baby Pete thinks there might be

a plate of cookies in the 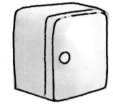 . After

breakfast, Baby Clarabelle will wash the

dishes in the  . She will leave the kitchen

clean and tidy by putting everything away

in the  when it is dry.

Sink

Cupboard

Refrigerator

Stove

Toaster

EATING

It is time for supper, and the Disney Babies want

to help set the table. Baby Goofy has found a

 and is beating on a saucepan with it,

like a drum. Baby Donald likes

and is bringing them up to the table. There is

plenty of milk in a big and Baby Mickey

is glad, because milk is his favorite drink. Baby

Daisy's job is to hand up the  and the

which goes on the left side of the plate, next to the

 . Now they are almost ready to eat.

Can you help set the table at your house ?

26

Pitcher

Salt and Pepper

Spoon

Plate

Fork

Napkin

IN OUR BEDROOM

It is nighttime, and the 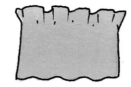 are closed

in Baby Minnie's bedroom. The babies are having

a  fight. Baby Minnie is excited

because her friends are staying overnight. She

jumps up on the  to throw a pillow at Baby

Pete. Baby Goofy is glad Baby Minnie didn't knock

over the  beside her bed. Otherwise, he

couldn't play with his toy car, because it would

be too dark. Now, the Babies are getting tired.

They are ready to climb under the clean white

 and go to sleep.

Pillow

Lamp

Bed

Curtains

Sheets

OUR BODIES

The Disney Babies are playing a guessing game

about the parts of their bodies. Baby Mickey

shows his to Baby Donald.

Baby Donald says, "Nose !" Baby Mickey touches

his . Then Baby Donald says, "Ear !"

Baby Daisy peeks around the corner. She waves

at everyone with her  , but the others

are so busy they don't notice her. Baby Gus is

combing the doll's  , and Baby

Clarabelle is tapping on Baby Minnie's .

Baby Minnie is holding her .

Hair

Hand

Ear

Nose

Foot

Arm

WHAT WE WEAR

Baby Minnie and Baby Mickey are playing

dress-up. Baby Mickey is wearing a big cowboy

 and boots, but he has to hold onto

the hat, or it will fall over his eyes. He has tried on

the bow 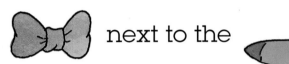 next to the  , but he

likes the bib with the sheriff's star better. The

 Baby Minnie has put on is too big,

but she likes the way it looks with her hair bow.

Her high-heeled  are so big that it

makes her laugh. Now who will put on that heavy

 that hangs in the closet ?

Coat

Hat

Shoes

Dress

Tie

Sock

IN OUR BATHROOM

Every night before they go to bed, the Disney

Babies take a bath. The  is so big that

Baby Horace and Baby Mickey can get in it at the

same time. Beside the tub is a pile of clean

to dry off with. Baby Donald has just finished his

bath and is sitting on the  while he

dries himself. Then he will brush his feathers with

the  . When they are bigger, the

Disney Babies will be able to go into the

that you can see in the mirror. But now they would

rather play with their boats in the tub.

Shower

Hairbrush

Bathtub

Bathmat

Towels

CLEANING UP

The Disney Babies are cleaning up their play room.

Baby Daisy is using an  to press her doll

clothes. Baby Gus was dusting, but the dust cloth

was sucked up by the  . Now Baby

Donald and Baby Gus are having a tug-of-war with

the vacuum to pull the dust cloth out. Baby Mickey

was trying to sweep with the  but it is

too big for him. He would rather play with Baby

Goofy, who is floating a toy boat in the .

Oops ! Some water has spilled on the floor. Maybe

Baby Mickey can mop it up with the  .

Iron

Vacuum Cleaner

Broom

Sponge

Bucket

IN OUR GARAGE

Baby Mickey and Baby Pete are in the garage

building a toy car. Baby Pete has found a hammer

in the 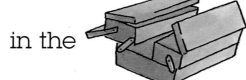 and is pounding in a wooden

peg. Baby Mickey holds another peg for him.

They have found some paint on the

over the workbench, but it is so high that a

grownup will have to climb the

to reach it. But the Babies had better move

their  out of the way.

Then, they will paint their car with the brush

on the  .

Ladder

Shelf

Workbench

Bicycle

Toolbox

OUR CAR

Baby Daisy has almost finished washing the car,

with help from Baby Clarabelle. The chrome

 is sparkling, and Baby Mickey has

turned the windshield  on and off to

be sure they are working for his trip. Baby Donald

has checked each for air. Now he is putting

the suitcase in the trunk. And Baby Minnie has

fastened her  so she will be safe in the

car. Of course, Baby Mickey has buckled his, too.

He feels very proud behind the  .

Have a good trip !

Wipers

Steering Wheel

Seatbelt

Bumper

Tire

TOOLS WE USE

Baby Gyro is very careful with his toolbox. But

his friends may use his tools if they ask. Baby

Gyro wants to tighten a bolt. He is using the

 , but he could also use the .

Baby Donald wants to pound a peg, so he has asked

if he may borrow the  .

But Baby Pete doesn't ask. He grabs the

 out of the toolbox and throws

everything else on the floor, even the  ,

with its very sharp teeth. Poor Baby Gyro! Now

he must put all the tools back into the toolbox.

Hammer

Wrench

Pliers

Saw

Screwdriver

SHAPES WE SEE

Different shapes are hiding all over Baby Mickey's

room, once you start to look for them. The round

base of the lamp is a ⬤ , and so are the big

dots on the curtains. Can you tell that Baby Mickey

is playing sheriff by the ★ on his bib ? The

toy box with the picture of a train on it is shaped

like a ▬ . The clown doll on the bed is

leaning against a pillow with an ⬭ shape,

and over it hangs a picture of a merry-go-round in a

■ frame. What's that Baby Gyro is cutting

out ? If it has three sides, it must be a ◁ .